Fatherly Advice

"A Father's Dreams, Hopes and Advice for His Sons"

Max Gerald Garoutte, MD

I0145512

Bryden Enterprises, Inc.

As iron sharpens iron, so one man sharpens another.

Published by
Bryden Enterprises, Inc.
San Antonio, Texas

Cover Design, Interior Design and Typesetting by
Bryden Enterprises, Inc in conjunction with Createspace

Publisher's Cataloging-in-Publication

Garoutte, Max Gerald,

Fatherly advice: " a father's dreams, hopes and advice for his
sons"/Max Gerald Garoutte.

p.cm.

ISBN 0-9746956-3-7

1.   Parental advice. 2. Christian living. 3. Self-help. 4.
Christian guidance. 5. Parental relationships. 1. Title
2.

Printed in the United States of America

DEDICATION

Dedicated to my earthly father, Max Wade Garoutte, Ed.D, Lt. Colonel (ret). A man who loved his children and grandchildren. A man who was a gentle warrior with a kind and generous spirit. A man who loved God.

And...dedicated to my Heavenly Father, who gives me strength when I need it and grace, love and mercy when I don't deserve them.

I look forward to the day that I can see you both.

To my three special sons:

Bryce, Tristan and Braden.

May you live lives of adventure, purpose, duty and honor.

I cannot live your lives for you, but I can share my experiences and wisdom with you.

You are all believers in the Almighty God.

With Him, you can do anything.

His path is not always straight but it is true.

Stay in His will.

And He will walk with you.

He will be your friend and protector.

He will love you intensely and unconditionally.

As I do.

CONTENTS

Acknowledgements

As I pass through middle age, and onto a new life stage, I am blessed and challenged by the wisdom and discernment for which I have prayed. Little did I know that when I asked for these gifts, that God would say, "yes." By granting me wisdom and discernment, he required me to pay a price through experiencing: intense love, betrayal, loss, deep sadness, depression, extraordinary physical and emotional pain-ALL because He loved me. I recognize that while my children mature into young adults, I will less-and-less be able to shelter them from the storms in their lives that will inevitably come. Releasing your child to the world in these dangerous times is frightening.

My wife and soul-mate, Meg, and I have tried to prepare our children to the best of our abilities using the resources that God has provided for us. Without her constant support, I could not be the man that I am. Her passion for life is extraordinary. She has been the finest example of a godly wife whose whole spirit is bathed in love and truth.

I am thankful that I have had the absolute honor to be a physician to my patients. In so many ways, they have inspired me and validated my career choice. While experiencing my career entering its twilight, I am thankful that God has allowed me to serve such a high calling as his "first assistant" in the healing of the ill.

I am grateful to Martie Conroy and Nancy Kemether for kindly reading and providing editorial support. Their input was invaluable.

To the readers of this book who have purchased it for themselves, or their children, <u>thank you</u>. A sizable portion of the revenue generated from sales will be donated to our company, *Play It Forward, Inc.* This company has a mission to provide spiritual life lessons to children through sports and the arts.

I thank my sons who have been patient with their old dad when he uttered advice, guidance and admonition- even when they didn't want it. Their tolerance of me has been exceptional. So, I offer this book to them, from their father who is aging, fallible and broken in so many ways. You, my sons, are the stars in my sky. May God bless you all.

Bryce, Tristan and Braden:

How I love you all! You are so precious and wonderful in such different and special ways. I have not always been the best example for you. Certainly, there have been times when I have modeled how NOT to be; whether it was intolerance, impatience, depression, anger or intemperance. But, I always loved you.

What an honor to be a dad to a son! God's path for me was much different than I ever expected or planned, but it was the right path. Just as I had to release my tight hold on two sons, I gained another. And now, you are three. It has been a joy to watch you grow. It has been painful to see you stumble, but it has been validating and encouraging to witness you getting up, brushing yourselves off and keep walking toward your goals and dreams. Within each one of you is a small kernel of me that I hope will flourish as it is watered by life's challenges and events. A godly father's dream is that his children will exceed his successes and avoid his downfalls. I challenge each of you to rise to your highest level and use God's gifts to the fullest. Don't waste them! They are precious and sometimes fleeting. You will be blessed with a limited number of opportunities in this life. Some that are given to you, but most that you create by hard work, diligence, direction and staying open to the possibilities.

Within each of you resides the Holy Spirit. How powerful is it to know that God lives within us! He WILL guide you if you call upon Him earnestly, honestly and patiently. He may not give you wealth, but He will always give you richness in family, friends, experiences and opportunities to serve. He will bless you with the utter joy of knowing that this life is temporal; however, one day He will call you to live with Him in eternal bliss.

So, we begin our journal of sagely and heartfelt advice from your dad. I speak directly to you with the hope that these words will sink deeply into your soul, sustain you in the hard times and give you hope and encouragement as you take this journey we call life.

With Eternal Heartfelt Love,   Dad

Adjust Your Binoculars

Where is your focus? I have encouraged each of you to have plans, aspirations and goals. They are the lifeblood that keeps all humans, but especially men: vital, engaged and productive. You cannot accomplish much without them. Remember, it is always difficult to bring the focus of your "binoculars" into crystal clear vision when goals are set far in the future. Your paths to your goals will rarely be straight. I want you to identify your goals and the reasons why you wish to achieve them. Why? Because your true purpose lies in the *reasons* that you wish to achieve these goals. *If you are unsuccessful in your achievement, many times it is because the reasons for setting your goals are not in God's will and directives to us.* Write down your goals and document the reasons that you wish to achieve them.

There is nothing wrong with obtaining wealth or material things, unless they become the center of your focus and they become the ultimate goal. *Wealth should be a byproduct of your activities, not a means to an end.* Take it from a dad who had everything and lost it. Wealth, fame, fortune and acquiring material things can be filled with a vacuous reality if these are your goals. Just look at all the celebrities who seemingly have "everything," but really have nothing in the end. Their fame and fortune seems to always fade. The "friends" that they have disappear when the money and the things money can buy are gone. In the end, they are left as empty, ugly shells of humanity. God taught me a great lesson when he allowed me to acquire material wealth, and then, lose it. Things aren't important. Godly relationships are.

So, focus on today. Vet the reasons for your goals against what will be pleasing to God. It will bring your goals into clarity and perspective. It will help you adjust your sights on goals that are worthy of God's blessing. It will allow you to see the important things in life-your family, your friends and your God.

Questions and Notes

1. *What are the reasons that binoculars were chosen versus a spyglass or telescope in this analogy?*
2. *When and why is it helpful to have someone you trust utilize their binoculars to have a vision of your goal?*
3. *What are your plans, aspirations and goals?*
4. *How often will you be using your binoculars while you make your journey to your goal?*
5. *What are your contingency plans if you have impediments to your goals?*
6. *What will you do if you achieve your goals only to lose them in the end?*
7. *How do you see your goals relating to family, friends and God?*
8. *Do you have goals of service, or just material acquisitions and position?*

The Two Golden Rules

There are two "Golden Rules" in life. One is from God and one is from man. My prayer is that you will understand the power of them both.

God's Golden Rule is that we live in relationship with all of our fellow human beings in a way that we would never do anything to them that we would not want done to ourselves. How powerful is that! As a society, can you imagine the power of this principle if we would ALL live it? Instead of fists, we would have open hands that would be willing to reach out and pick up our fellow man. We would open our fists and release our time, effort and resources to help people. We would show our love by action, not just empty words. Can you imagine if every country, every faction of society would release their control of their time, money and resources to show generosity toward those in need? Can you imagine a time when there would be no more wars or famine? *Following God's Golden Rule requires personal sacrifice and a willingness to turn selfishness into selflessness. Jesus is the ultimate example of selflessness.* Those who realize the power of this principle will be blessed beyond their wildest dreams.

Man's Golden Rule is "he who has the gold makes the rules." With great wealth, comes great power. As aspiring leaders, this may sound intoxicating to you, but heed my words. *With great power and wealth, comes great responsibility.* So few of our leaders have followed God's Golden Rule, but have chosen to follow the evil one's rule. Wealth, and its associated power, are corrupting to most humans. Look at the number of wealthy businessmen and celebrities who fall under the devil's control and directives.

If God choses to bless you with the "gold," understand that He has chosen you to be challenged to do the right thing with your resources. Your nemesis will be yourself, and the devil will be constantly whispering in your ear. Do more. Make more. Use your gold for power. Use your power to control. If you choose the evil one's path, you will fall and you will lose that which was not yours in the first place. All things including money are God's. I don't discourage you from living a life that may result in God's blessings including money. But, you must understand that if you acquire money and power, you must call upon His direction and follow His rules. You must share your money and power in a way that will reflect the true Golden Rule....God's Golden Rule.

Questions and Notes

1. *If you become the man who has the gold and makes the rules, how will you make this compatible with God's Golden Rule?*
2. *Power and wealth are intoxicating and addicting. If God choses for you to have them, how will you counteract these effects?*
3. *Are you prepared to release your control associated with the acquisition of wealth and power if God chooses a different path for you?*

Great Men Listen

Each of you has been born with the gift of conversation and interaction. For that, I am thankful. You certainly didn't get these attributes from your dad. Because I am an extreme introvert, I have often had my shyness confused for aloofness or conceit. Sadly, this was a false impression that I could never really overcome. This trait certainly impeded my success in some areas, but it was a reflection of my personality-bad or good. Thankfully, you are all outgoing and capable of interactive conversation in many ways. I am happy for you because you will have many more friends than I ever had, and there will be doors of opportunity open for you that never were available for me. However, you must be careful when you express your outgoing personalities so that they reflect interest in others. I encourage you to interact with people in an engaging and inquisitive way. *The power of turning the "I's into You's" cannot be overstated.* People like to talk about themselves. You have much to learn from others. You only need to ask. Although a conversation requires a give and take, you can control the direction and outcome of a conversation by following the 3 to 1 principle. *You ask three questions for every one that you answer.* When you meet a new person, look them squarely in the eye, smile genuinely, shake their hand and ask their name. Use their name in your first question to them. The power of hearing one's name in a question expresses interest in the individual that is tangible and real. It demonstrates genuine interest.

We live in a tangential, throw-away society where we are marginalized and depersonalized. Personalizing an individual, and using their name in conversation, can result in an immediate connection that will lead to a comfort level which might take hours to accomplish otherwise. By asking three questions for every one that you are answering gives you an opportunity to convert the "I's into You's."

As future leaders, you will need to develop powerful, sustained relationships with individuals who can work with you to accomplish your dreams and goals. No man is an island. I had to learn this the hard way. You will build better plans with the assistance of wisdom and input of others. It is in our nature to help each other if we feel comfortable in our relationships. If you show new acquaintances genuine interest, and you develop trust with them, you will be better leaders and better men.

Questions and Notes

1. *Hearing and listening are interrelated but not synonymous processes. How do you differentiate between the two?*
2. *Who are your mentors with whom you would chose to listen?*
3. *What separates random conversation from focused conversation?*
4. *You will meet many people from different backgrounds and orientations. How will you learn to listen to them even if you don't agree with their viewpoints?*

Whisper Your Words; Let Your Actions Shout

True power to influence comes from your actions, not words. We live in a divisive and confrontational world. Yet, the power of a quiet word cannot be overstated. Paradoxically, people will listen more intently if you speak quietly, calmly and confidently. You can control and deescalate most confrontations by lowering your tone and volume. By quietly speaking, I am saying that you speak from confidence, not timidity. There are really very few instances in human interaction in which yelling will accomplish as much as a whisper. Whispers (figuratively) impart closeness and a drawing in. Yelling repels. I have certainly been guilty of violating this admonition in my own life and it has taken five decades to learn the power of the whisper. My hope is that you will learn it now. It will serve you well.

Sadly, we live in a duplicitous and corrupt world. Remember, people are judging you more by your actions than your words. Your words and actions must breathe truth and an unwavering conviction to do "the right thing." You must demonstrate what you are saying to gain their confidence. In fact, the Bible calls us into action. Even our prayers should lead to actions. *If what you are saying, and how you are saying it, cannot be reflected in your concurrent and consistent actions, then you are not being true to yourselves, others and most importantly...God.* God will judge you by your actions and their consequences. The fruit that you bear will reveal the purity of your soul.

Questions and Notes

1. *How and when to words become actions?*

2. *When are their times when it is better to let your actions be your words?*

3. *Your words and actions can provide a "window to your heart." How will adjust your conduct so that when God was looking through the window, he will be pleased?*

Make Believers Your Friends and Your Acquaintances Believers

Because of your physical beauty, your engaging personalities and the opportunities that you have; you will all have many, many friends in your lives. I encourage you to seek out friends who are believers in Christ. Not to the exclusion of others, but to empower you to reach out to acquaintances who are non-believers. Christians are imperfect and most of us can be hypocritical to a point. However, true believers have an understanding of the "playbook." You can relate to them on a level that non-believers cannot understand until you show them by your actions and words. The Bible instructs us to seek out the "equally yoked" for relationship especially in the marital relationship...

We are only humans, but God lives in us through the Holy Spirit. There is strength in numbers. In your life you will have many acquaintances, but fewer true friends. Let your life create a sense of wonder and longing in the non-believing acquaintance. If the non-believer is repelled, understand that God does not expect us to "pick green fruit." It is likely that the acquaintance is living an ungodly life and may have the devil strongly influencing him or her. The more engaging or beautiful a non-believer is; the more that you should approach the individual with extreme caution for the devil is the father of lies and the great deceiver. Influence should come from God and His children, not non-believers. Don't misunderstand me. I am not saying that you shouldn't engage and interact with non-believers. You should. But, do so cautiously, prayerfully and understand that you accept great responsibility to let your thoughts, words and actions be reflective of your belief system. The devil has his minions who are doing his bidding. Take care. Be discernful. Stay close to those who know the Truth that resides in you.

Questions and Notes

1. What are the ways that you have the power of influence over your acquaintances?

2. How will you interact with non-believers in a way that will not be offensive, but will also allow you to avoid bad influences?

3. Name some opportunities that might present themselves with non-believers so that you could politely share your faith?

4. We are all blessed with the capacity for intuition. How will you use your intuition to avoid bad situations?

Live a Life Worthy of Watching Because HE Is Watching

In this world of social media, YouTube and instant access, we are increasingly vulnerable to public scrutiny and judgment. Over the past years, you have been greatly cautioned about photos, observations, statements and conversations that you put out into the cyber world. How many opportunities have been lost? How many relationships have been spoiled? All because of stupid and thoughtless moment when something was placed on an internet social networking page for all to see. It is forever captured. Unlike God who knows our deficiencies and is willing to forgive our transgressions if we ask; the world does not offer the same forgiveness and grace. In the past, our sins have been private for the most part and only known to a few family and friends generally. With God's forgiveness, we could wipe the slate clean. I believe that there is great danger in using social networking and you need to be especially careful what you type into a social networking page or text on your phone. *God has a selective memory. He forgets and forgives for the asking.* The evil one never forgets. Human beings are fallen. They have the power to forgive, but rarely have the power to forget.

You should attempt to live each day as one that you would be happy to replay for your family, friends and your God. You will never be perfect, but you will be forgiven.

Questions and Notes

1. *Have you ever submitted information, photos or opinions on social media that you wish to retract? If so, how would you accomplish this?*

2. *Do you have someone to whom you have done wrong and need to apologize? If so, why haven't you done so?*

3. *What will you do if you apologize to someone and they do not accept your apology?*

4. *Sometimes, the hardest thing to do is to forgive yourself. Have you had this issue? If so, how do you plan to begin the process of forgiveness?*

5. *What is the "process of forgiveness?"*

6. *How will you let your actions demonstrate your words when you are seeking, or accepting forgiveness?*

Give Honor to Others

You have all been taught the magical power of using "sir and ma'am" when you address those who are senior to you in age and/or authority. As you get older, you will find a comfort in addressing those who are younger and who are subordinate to you in this way. Why? Because, it is a reflection of honoring all men and women. Our society has seen a progressive degradation of common courtesy and propriety. I call upon you, as the leaders of the future, to reverse this trend in your life. Each and every human being is of special value to God. Giving honor to others reflects your understanding of this.

I challenge you to tell me when there was a time when you showed honor and respect to someone when it did not improve the interpersonal interaction. *You are not lowering yourself, but elevating the other person.* I hope that you will carry on the family tradition of showing honor to others as you raise your children. It is powerful and it is pleasing to God.

Questions and Notes

1. *Why is it suggested that you address children as "sir or ma'am?"*

2. *Have you ever experienced the power of showing honor and respect to others?*

3. *The world appears to be a more disrespectful place than in the past. Why is this? How can we change it? Why is it important to change it?*

The Power of Team

No man is an island, no matter how good you are. This is a tough concept for some high achievers to grasp. The sooner that you understand the value and power of human interaction as it relates to a common purpose; the sooner that *you will be able to create a synergy of purpose that is created out of relationship.* <u>We are created for relationship and purpose. Without these, life has no meaning</u>. You cannot fully define your purpose without God's influence... and the help of others. You have all been participants of team sports. To me, it didn't matter what the sport was, only that you participate in interaction with other people toward a common goal-winning. Team sports teach that everyone's contribution counts. It teaches that there are few leaders and many followers...and you need both to succeed. All my sons have the capacity to lead. Your upbringing and educational pathways have prepared you to lead. Whether you choose this great responsibility is between God and you. He may call you to lead. He may not. Either way, throughout your life, you will be bonding in teamwork for a common purpose. Only

God, Jesus and the Holy Spirit can thrive independently and curiously, despite Their omnipotence, They have chosen a team as well. Why shouldn't we?

Questions and Notes

1. Why do people choose to live on "islands?"
2. Is the safety of an island real or imagined?
3. How are relationships, opportunities and purpose interrelated?
4. How can the Holy Trinity help you overcome shyness or fear?

Seek Wisdom and Discernment

Isn't it interesting that when God offered to grant Solomon any of the gifts that he chose wisdom and discernment? Curiously, despite his wisdom, his choices and lifestyle did not always reflect these traits. However, he was smart enough to realize the great power that comes with wisdom and discernment which not coincidently gave him great riches. Like all gifts from God, you must use them for His purpose.

As I have grown older, I have learned the power and strength that come from wisdom and discernment. Unfortunately, in my case, these gifts have come at the expense of making bad choices and decisions and feeling the searing reality of their outcomes. As a parent, I pray often for your protection and that you will make good decisions. I am confident that with God's truth expressed in His Holy Scriptures, and with prayerful consideration, you can realize wisdom and discernment beyond your years. *Your decisions and their outcomes can define you in the world's eyes.* Only God knows your soul. So, in this world, making good and godly decisions are paramount to success.

The wisest men are men who have lived a full life and learned from their experiences. They are men who are constantly inquisitive and are on a journey for truth. They are men who will seek godly counsel and wise mentors. Wisdom can be a baton passed from one to another if you listen carefully. Discernment is more challenging as it requires you to weigh options and opinions. With God's help and the assistance of His followers, you can obtain both. And with both, you have limits that only God can set!

Questions and Notes

1. *If God chose to grant you any single gift, what would yours be? Why?*

2. *Why do you think that Solomon, despite all of his wisdom, made bad choices?*

3. *How do you think that you are defined in the world by your decisions and their outcomes? Does God define you the same way? If not, why?*

4. *Have you selected life mentors to help you on your journey? Who are they and why did you choose them?*

Dare Not To Compare

The act of comparison is the devil's workshop. God isn't comparing one of his children against another. The evil one does. The outcome of comparison is always negative for somebody. As Christians, we are called not to judge. We are commanded to lift each other up and to understand that we are all equally valuable in the eyes of our God. We live in a world of seven billion people-all unique and special in God's eyes. You can take me at my word that there will always be someone stronger, more handsome, richer, more popular than you are if you choose to compare yourself to others. Yes, there is no doubt that each of my sons has been blessed with many gifts, attributes and talents. However, these are God's gifts to you and He does not want you to defile and degrade His gifts by comparing yourself to others. Remember, we are created for relationship.

The concept of comparison is born out of the world's necessity for competition. There is nothing wrong with competition for a common goal. There are goals that only certain people are meant to achieve. Competition can make us better and prepare us to serve God. However, your challenge is to compete in a way that you are utilizing your skills, gifts and talents to their maximum benefit, but not in a way that is demeaning to others. Let your actions and its resulting success speak for itself. Comparison serves no purpose and your joy is in victory that is achieved without stepping on others. *Invite God to help you be the best that YOU can be and to accomplish your goals without need for comparison.* If you follow this admonition, you have my promise that you will accomplish more and you will realize much greater joy and satisfaction from your achievements. Conversely, if you choose a life of comparison that is the evil one's way, you will never be satisfied. What is your choice?

Questions and Notes

1. *To who are you comparing yourself? Why?*

2. *Why are comparisons the devil's tool?*

3. *There is no comparison to that which is unique? How are you truly unique?*

4. *What is the difference between good, healthy competition and bad competition?*

Fame and Other Fleeting Things

When you are young, fame is often defined by celebrity. Athletes and actors tend to be role models of the young. Children see these individuals as being special because of their talents, beauty, money and power. When you grow older, you will realize that fame is fleeting, and rarely, is it used for God's glory. The temptations are ubiquitous. This why so many famous people fall into the evil one's hands and die prematurely. The majority of the rich, powerful and famous are living empty, godless lives. Why? Because, the quest for fame is generally based on selfish reasons. Fame is the devil's tool to destroy, and ultimately defame. *It is the devil's ploy to use celebrities to do his bidding by encouraging others that they should strive for worldly things, not the blessings of God.* In the end, how many truly happy famous people do you believe that there are?

I am confident that each of my sons is blessed with gifts and talents that may lead to worldly fame. Nonetheless, it is my prayer that you understand that fame can be more of a curse than a blessing. Temptation, loss of privacy, public scrutiny often accompanies fame. The most severe perturbation of the famous is when they perceive themselves as god-like. Then, the devil truly has won.

I want my sons to be famous in a different way. They may never sign an autograph, but they will sign checks for the poor. They may not be on television, or in the movies, but they will be living a life worth watching. Their wives will adore and respect them and their children will revere them even knowing all their imperfections. This is true fame in God's eyes.

Questions and Notes

1. *How many famous celebrities and athletes can you list who have become infamous? What do you think the cause of their infamy was?*

2. *Why do people want to become famous? How is this contrary to Jesus's teachings?*

3. *What is the turning point when people with fame start considering themselves god-like?*

4. *What are the downsides of fame?*

The Power of Coincidence in God's World

I hope that you live your lives with your eyes wide open, and in constant vigilance that God is with you. He shows Himself in subtle ways that only the discerning Christian can appreciate. I don't believe that there is such a thing as coincidence. It is just God's way of smiling on you and wondering if you understand that He just touched you. Coincidence many times reflects God's validation or approval. It can reflect His mutual joy with and for us.

Recently, I was giving God thanks and appreciation for the opportunity to enjoy the beauty and peace that is present at our Colorado home as I was on the way to the house from the airport. He responded by releasing a falling star. I am sure that this was God's tear of joy knowing that I appreciate his gifts. Just before Braden had his Eagle Scout ceremony, I was on the deck of our mountain home watching the river and what flew over the river from west to east...a bald eagle! Was it just coincidence, or was it validation of that which is good and wholesome and brings honor to Him?

For being such an awesome and powerful God, it is amazing how subtle and quietly that God can speak to us. In my eyes and in God's eyes, all my sons are awesome. If it is in His will, they may be powerful leaders. If that is one of the challenges and gifts that God gives them, I hope that they speak with a sense of authority and strength-quietly and with wonderment of that which is good.

Questions and Notes

1. *Have you ever experienced "coincidence?" If so, do you think that God had a role in the occurrence? What was His reason for allowing the coincidence?*

For Crying Out Loud

Human emotion is a gift from God. Of course, happiness and joy are easy to understand as coming from God. Grief, anger, pain, sadness are more challenging to accept as "gifts." Even Jesus wept and became angry. There is nothing wrong with righteous indignation. Since I have become a father, I have noticed my propensity for tears in sadness, and in great joy. Frankly, as a man, it is embarrassing at times, especially when I am so overcome with emotion that it is hard to stem the tears. However, I am learning to accept this phenomenon as a validation of my utter joy and overwhelming peace that I have when I know that God is with me. He has blessed me when I deserved neither mercy, nor grace. I have come to the realization that when I meet God in heaven, I will not be on my feet dancing with praise, but on my knees, crying tears of joy and gratefulness for His unconditional love for me.

It is my perspective that my sons have a bit more control over tearful emotions. This should prevent you from needless personal embarrassment. However, it is my prayer that you not be afraid to cry tears of joy and sadness. *Tears, whether shed in happiness or despair, cleanse the soul and validate our humanity.*

Questions and Notes

1. *Are you embarrassed to cry in public? Why? Do you think that this matters to God?*

2. *How often do you cry tears of sadness versus tears of joy?*

3. *The emotions that invoke tears are God-given. What is his purpose behind tears of joy and tears of sorrow?*

Money Matters...Or Does It?

Each of my sons has been brought up in a home of abundance. You have had a childhood that was only in my dreams when I was young. God has blessed us in many ways. Throughout time, society has been reliant on individual production and has assigned value to tasks in exchange for money. The money, in turn, was used to purchase goods and services. Jesus spent much time preaching about money. The bottom line is, *are you holding your money, or is it holding you?* The Bible commands us to work and be productive. In these days, we are compensated for the value of our production and services with money. The problem lies with after we have paid for a "daily bread," what will we do with the rest of our resources? Clearly, the Bible commands us to bring our "first fruits" to the church for God's bidding. This is a concept that challenges most of us-including me. As I have matured, I am realizing that the concept of tithing, or bringing your first fruits, is really a way that God is trying to teach us to release our money for the benefit of His kingdom. More importantly, it is a demonstration of our faith that He will provide us sufficiently if we are productive. If you really ponder the act of tithing, you understand the act is the lesson. He doesn't need our money, our things or resources. He owns them all anyway.

I have not been the perfect example at times. However, I am doing better with regard to "releasing my things." As a physician, I have donated hundreds of thousands of dollars in the value of my time toward the indigent just as I am called to do. Yet, I can always do more. *Don't let the size of your bank account define you-it doesn't ...at least in God's eyes. How you use your resources will define you.* This is God's lesson. Give to the church and keep an account available that is for helping others. Our Heavenly Father will present the opportunities to you in His time and you will be a blessing to others as God is a blessing to us. You will know the true joy of giving when you become adults and have children. Only then, will you understand the pure joy that it is to give gifts to your children, just as God has given gifts to us.

Questions and Notes

1. *How will you react if it is God's choice that you have a standard of living that is less than when you grew up as a child?*

2. *If you have no money to donate, what else can you give to those in need?*

3. *How do you value your time? Does society value it the same way?*

4. *If you aren't blessed with the spirit of generosity, how can you overcome this so that you can honor God?*

5. *How does having a fancy car or a huge home affect the public's perception of you? How do these things affect God's perception of you?*

6. *How do you know when you have enough?*

Create Your Masterpiece

You don't need to be an artist or an artisan to be creative. We have two sides of our brains for a reason. This is another of God's gifts. The power to calculate and to reason, and the power to create. I think many people are discouraged from creating because they are worried about failure or comparison. Unfortunately, there is a bias against creativity. Creative people are portrayed as strange and unproductive in our society. Who cares? Creativity is another way to express yourself, whether in words, arts or crafts. Creativity stretches us, and is a place of peaceful resolution. It gives rise to a sense of accomplishment and is a healthy release from daily tensions. You need not worry. Most of us will never make a dime from our creations, but that is not the point anyway. Over the years, I have chosen to express myself through prose, poetry, music and art. Frankly, none of my efforts are particularly good. However, they have been immensely therapeutic. It has given me joy, satisfaction and a sense of accomplishment. I feel no pressure when I am creating because I have no expectations of profiting financially from my efforts. Mostly, only my soul will benefit. Maybe, one day my grandchildren or great grandchildren will find one of my books, or articles, or paintings, or poems, or songs, and they will gain insight into a man that they may have never known.

The energy and passion that you can release in your creations is a miniscule reflection of the great energy, love and passion that God had when he created us and the world upon which we live.

Perhaps, you will have a few admirers of your work in your family and friends. You may even see your work reach a level of appreciation to the general public. However, it is likely that you will have a fan club of only one... God...and that is enough.

Questions and Notes

1. *How are you to create your masterpiece? What areas of creativity do you wish to pursue and why haven't you pursued them yet?*

2. *How do you place a value on creative outlets? Why is it important to have them?*

3. *Do you need to be an artist or musician to be creative? If not, what other ways can you reflect your creativity?*

Respect for Love <u>AND</u> Love for Respect

      Having suffered through the pain of divorce, one of my most intimate and heartfelt prayers for my sons, is that you will find a godly wife who is willing to give you the honor and respect that the Bible commands. Likewise, you will have the duty to love her as Christ loved the church. This is Biblical. It is true and it is the one best hope for you to marry once and marry right. You have all experienced the pain and disruption of broken marriages that ended in divorce. I pray with intensity that you can only imagine that you will be patient and thoughtful in finding a wife. You will have a pre-requisite that she is a Christ follower and that she will commit her life to you in such a way that she will show you respect when your actions make it difficult. Just as you are called to show her unconditional love when it may not be easy. I pray that she will be a true partner with you and that she will complement you by giving your support and encouragement when you need it. I pray that she will learn to forgive you when it is hard to do. I pray that she will put God first in her life, and you and only you, will be second. I pray that she will honor you no matter what you do, or how much you make. I pray that she will always have your back no matter what. I pray that if you fall upon hard times that both of you will agree to get outside Christian counseling to help you through the rough times...and trust me, there will be some. I pray that she will never show disrespect for you with family or friends even if your actions don't deserve it. I pray she will be thankful for you and for what you provide. I pray that you will love your wife with an intensity that only God can explain. I pray that you will be faithful in heart and actions to your wife. I pray that you will provide for your family in a way that they have comfort and their daily bread. I pray that you put your wife second only to God. I pray that you never compromise your relationship to make another buck or achieve another empty accomplishment. I pray that you support your wife in a way that she will feel honored regardless of whether she chooses to work outside the home or in the home. I pray that you are able to provide for your family in a way so that your wife can work in the home with the children and can be there during their formative years. I pray that you will let nothing come between you and your wife and you will always cherish the sanctity of the marital relationship. I pray that you will not make the mistakes that your parents made. I pray that you will honor the marital covenant to the end of your lives. Forever together may you be. Amen

Questions and Notes

1. *What is the intended message in Ephesians 5:21-33?*

2. *Why do you believe that husbands and wives have so much difficulty adhering to scripture as it relates to love and respect?*

3. *Why does the Bible state that you should be equally yoked with your spouse? Why is this important?*

4. *What is the difference between submission and respect?*

5. *How many ways can a husband demonstrate his love for his wife?*

6. *How are you to respond to your spouse if you do not receive love or respect?*

7. *Is it really possible for a human being to have unconditional love? Justify your answer.*

Let God's Sun (Son) Shine Through You

You have been given the gift of life by a Creator who knew your name in the womb. You have accepted Christ as your Lord and Savior. By doing so, you will join your Heavenly Father and your earthly parents in the eternal perfection of heaven.

Ha! Isn't it great that everything else after that is just icing on the proverbial cake we call life. To have fellowship with God as a Christian is so powerful. As a Christian, I can see God's aura enveloping other Christians especially when we are speaking of matters that are important to Him. Don't be afraid to let your life's convictions shine! If you live a godly life, you will have non-believers wondering what and who you are. God prefers not to have slackers, or ne'er do wells, on His team. You are recruiter for Him. Let your actions show it. Be humble. Speak carefully and without judgment. Judgment is in His purview, not yours.

My sons have the power and responsibility to influence for the good of God and His purpose. *We may never be ordained, but we are expected to minister. You may not preach, but you may teach by your example and actions.* You don't need a pulpit to evangelize, but your character and demeanor will speak volumes to the joy of being one of God's children.

Don't let the evil one convince you that it is wrong to live out your faith. You don't need to be brash or offensive. *You can demonstrate your faith through your actions and by letting the aura of God's intense love and blessings shine through your soul.*

Questions and Notes

1. *Have you ever been overwhelmed by a sense of presence of the Holy Spirit? When?*

2. *Have you ever sensed the indwelling presence of the Holy Spirit in another person?*

3. *How can you demonstrate your faith in a way that will be engaging and not offensive to a non-believer?*

4. *How can you make people want what you have as it relates to your faith and relationship with Christ?*

Seek Out God-Loving Mentors

Each of my sons will likely enter a very competitive business environment regardless of your vocation. I cannot stress enough the importance of seeking out Christian mentors. I stress the importance that your mentors love Christ because there are many teachers of false doctrine in this world. They are the "nice guys finish last" type. You should start a file on your mentors and document their talents and specialties. Most accomplished Christian men welcome the opportunity to share their knowledge, wisdom and experience with a fellow believer.

You can compete successfully without stepping on others, lying or doing "zero sum" business deals. The most joy that I have is doing business transactions with people who want everyone to benefit. "Taking scalps" in business is for people who have low self- esteem and feel inadequate. Confident businessmen conduct business in a way that they don't burn bridges. They can meet a collaborator or competitor on the street; look them in the eye and know that they were honorable and forthright. Beware of the "go along to get along" crowd. This ALWAYS leads to compromise...many times in your ethics and morals. Don't be afraid to walk away from a bad business deal. If you are active in business, you will have many, many more deals never transpire over those that come to fruition. Whenever possible, try to build in an altruistic component to your business deals. Remember, it is only with God's bidding and support that you are even able to close the deal. Give Him some acknowledgement by helping others.

Questions and Notes

1. *How do you counter someone who tells you that "nice guys finish last?"*

2. *Name some individuals that you know that believe that "nice guys finish last" or that compete in a way that there must always be a loser.*

3. *Have you ever competed with someone in a way that you would feel uncomfortable if you met that person in a social setting? Why? How could you have changed the situation?*

4. *Sometimes the best business deals are the ones that don't get done. Have you had this experience? If so, do you think that God had a purpose in this "failure?"*

5. *How do you align your goals with God's goals for you in the business environment?*

Play It Forward

Several years ago, we created the company, *Play It Forward, Inc.* The goal was to teach Christian life lessons through sports and the arts. We have had a good start, but I challenge all of my sons to continue the program. Although your mother and I may have time to tangentially assist with the project, the hard work of formation of the company and establishing the mission has already been accomplished. You have been given so many talents and skills that you can apply to this effort. There is no need to reinvent the wheel. You only need to apply your time, effort and aptitude. The sky is the limit and you are in a position to help thousands of children.

One of the main concepts behind *Play It Forward* is people helping people in a way that is instructive with hope that those that are helped will help others one day. It is a way of modeling behavior that honors God and creates an environment of community and relationship. It is giving a hand up, not a hand out, to people in need.

You are each honing your various gifts in your training for your vocations and your avocations. As natural leaders, you are in a unique position to influence others and to share your gifts with others. We have created a platform from which you can do great things if you so choose.

Your parents will certainly be available to you for advice and support. It is our hope that you appreciate the foundation and opportunities that you have been given and that you will "play it forward" to others.

Questions and Notes

1. *Do you have passions or gifts that would allow you to "Play It Forward" to someone else?*

2. *The consequences of our good deeds are sometimes never known to us. Without positive feedback, why should we continue to press forward with our service to others?*

3. *What are the ways that you can serve others to foster the concept of community and relationship to others?*

Hard Lessons Learned the Hard Way

Sadly, my competitive nature and upbringing has made it difficult over the years for me to gracefully "turn the other cheek" as Jesus instructs us to do. I always perceived this to be a show of weakness. Frankly, I despise bullies. Unfortunately, you are going to run into them in all walks of life. You may have the misfortune of dealing with nefarious and corrupt business associates. You will have people attack, condemn and assault you. Your impulse will be to fight. I plead with you to take a breath. Sleep on your decisions. Seek out wise counsel, and whenever possible, walk away from acrimonious situations. It may bruise your ego, but in the end, you will be much ahead. *God's role, not yours, is to be the Avenger.*

It has taken my over fifty years to learn from the error of my ways. I am not sure even now that if a bad situation would arise that I wouldn't resort to my old ways of fighting and retaliation. I can only tell you that you will save countless thousands of dollars, and weeks of lost sleep, if you choose to take the high road. Remember, God is in your corner. He has your back. He is a God of love, not conflict. And... *vengeance shall be His, in His time and in His way.* As for you, cut your ties and release it to Him. You will be better off for it. He will bless you in way that will give you more satisfaction than any act of revenge....and He will give you the consolation and peace that passes all understanding-especially in times of adversity.

Questions and Notes

1. *How do you react to bullies? How should you react to them?*

2. *What are ways to diffuse conflict?*

3. *How do you release anger and the desire for retribution against your enemies?*

4. *How do you counteract the nefarious and evil in a way that would be pleasing to God?*

There Is Comfort in Consistency

Some people define others who are consistent in their beliefs, morals, lifestyles and relationships as boring. Beware! Those are the crazy ones! In the process of becoming mature men, it is my hope and desire that your personalities, lifestyles and beliefs will become stable, firm and based on unwavering convictions. Of course, the main stabilizing influence is our belief in Christ and the directions provided in scripture. This is a blueprint for success. Beyond that, you will be shaped by others who have influenced you-positively and negatively. You will be formed by how you have responded to adversity. Hopefully, you will not be strongly influenced by worldly trends, mainstream media or false teachers.

During your lifelong growth process, I encourage you to keep a diary and write down what makes you a special individual. In the privacy of a diary, you can do this without being fearful of being judged. This is a workbook for just you and God. Then, write down your goals-long and short term. What is your ideal job, family and wife? What do you see as your potential for contributing to society? Finally, write down the kind of man that you will need to become to achieve your goals. Be comprehensive and thoughtful. Filter your perspective through the truth of the Gospel. This is your mold, or pattern, if you will. It is a hard exercise, but it will serve you well. Don't worry about the rough edges, your Heavenly Father and the Holy Spirit will polish them out for you.

Remember, the truth shall set you free, and always be true to God...as well as yourself. God likes winners and he wants you to succeed. You can be His best advertisement! The most consistent Man on earth was Jesus Christ. The Pharisees constantly tried to trip Him up. He ultimately paid the supreme price...His death on the cross. People are drawn to individuals who are rock solid and consistent in all they do. Surprises are for birthday parties and anniversaries. Solid, unmovable, reliable, consistent truth is what people crave more than ever. Doors will open. Opportunities will present themselves. Interactive alignment with other truth seekers will happen. The evil one's minions will be repelled like vampires to a cross by

the Christ followers who are true to themselves and God
and consistent in their ways.

Questions and Notes

1. *Why is consistency considered boring or unfashionable in today's society?*

2. *Why is their inefficiency that accompanies inconsistency?*

3. *How will being consistent help you achieve your goals?*

4. *What areas of your character demand consistency for you to be a good servant to God?*

The Joy of Coaching

One of the best experiences that I ever had in my adult life was coaching my sons and other kids. The sense of satisfaction and accomplishment was enormous. Each of you has talents or skills; teach them to kids! Each of you have invested your time in different sports and have achieved success. This is your opportunity to "Play It Forward." To a young child, their coach can be very influential. This gives you an opportunity to demonstrate the benefits of teamwork and personal development.

When I was in eighth grade at my new school, I tried out for the basketball team. Being a pre-pubertal, pudgy, short-guy, my chances of making the team were slim. Despite being cut from the basketball team the year before at another school, I made the team! I was clearly the worst guy on the team, but one day, my coach saw me make an uncharacteristically good move on one of the star players on our team. He blew his whistle to stop the practice and said, "Garoutte. That was an awesome move. You're starting the next game!" The next game was against the school that had cut me from the team the year prior. We beat them by over twenty points even though I didn't contribute much. My coach had no idea about the significance of that game to me...but God did. My coach's belief in me sustained me for many years when I was faced with adversity.

I had the blessing of coaching Bryce for many years in both recreational and select baseball. What a joy! I recognized the chance to not only instruct the boys in the fundamentals, but to give them weekly Scripture-based life lessons. In essence, I was working Sunday school into a baseball practice! I am not sure if all of the parents liked my approach, but it didn't matter-God did. As you mature, you will find that your legacy can live on in the lives that you touch. Most of the time, we will never know until we get to heaven and sit down with God in the great media room in the sky to review our life's work. You have the power to influence positively and productively as a coach. Use it!

I know that winning the National Championship with Bryce's team was God's validation of my work. Perhaps, it was God's recognition of a means to an end, and it may have been His way of telling me that this chapter in my life was complete. I only know that for all my days I will look back at those times with great satisfaction.

Although I had a chance to coach Braden, it was limited through separation and divorce. This remains a regret that I will always have, and probably never fully understand. However, I am eternally grateful that God placed the desire and perseverance in his heart to allow him to achieve the rank of Eagle Scout!

I only had one chance to coach Tristan's baseball team...as a fill-in coach. Tristan's coaches were out of town and I had three hours to work with his YMCA team. During that time, I briefly re-experienced the joy of coaching. We saw boys hit who had been hitless and win when they were winless. What a blessing to experience God's validation through small feats! May you one day experience them too.

Questions and Notes

1. *What are areas in which you can teach or coach?*

2. *What are the principles that you wish to instill into your students or players?*

3. *Both positively and negatively, how can you change a kid's life by coaching him?*

4. *Do you have a teacher or coach who influenced you? Who? Why?*

5. *How do you balance competition to win with other life lessons learned in competitive sports?*

Plan to Work and Work Your Plan

This is a paraphrase of a famous "Meg quote" when she was in the corporate business world. It is an acknowledgement of the importance of thinking ahead, and then, working toward your goal. There are many people in life who function at a level of what I call, "point to point with no map." This is my way of saying that they are not thinking ahead to what their next move will be, and more importantly, what will be their contingency plans if the direction, or rules of the game, change. I cannot emphasize enough the importance of visualizing the game board of life in a way that you would approach a chess board. Identify your goal, develop your path, and then, think through the possible adaptations that you may need to make if your plans don't succeed initially. Most people become stymied if they hit roadblocks. You need to be prepared to hurdle, avoid or traverse the things that hinder your progress. One of the lessons taught in the martial arts is to use your opponent's energy to give you power and momentum. You can do this in life. Opposition has an energy force that if you always fight against it, will fatigue you, and perhaps, defeat you. However, if you learn to deflect the negative energy, you will continue your progress. *Preparation for adversity will allow you to repel and deflect problems and impediments. Problems will give rise to opportunities and opportunities will optimize your likelihood for success.*

Questions and Notes

1. *How will preparation and planning benefit you when you are establishing your goals? What will be the consequences if you fail to adequately "map out your journey?"*

2. *Do you know people who seem to be meandering through life? What are the consequences of this haphazard approach?*

3. *If you hit roadblock along your journey toward a goal, how will you adapt and who will you call upon to help you?*

4. *How can you make the negative energy of adversity or evil work to your advantage while you are pursuing your goals?*

Build a Nest

No matter where you are, build a nest. Nesting is the term that I refer to when you have a place of comfort that contains your furniture, a car, and your photos, etc., that connect you to your past. In the nest, you surround yourself with family that you know that you can trust.

We live in an itinerant world. This is unfortunate because stability and tradition has been a benchmark of our society in the past. No longer do people build a house and live in the same neighborhood for fifty years. Rarely, do doctors hang their shingle out at single office, only to take it down forty years later when their careers are finished. We are depriving ourselves of the comfort and peace of continuity for the opportunity to have more and better. Although advancing toward your dream house or perfect job is commendable, don't be sad if God calls you to stay where you are to build your nest.

I have always marveled at your Aunt Gee and Uncle Dennis. They lived in this way. They built their nest as young adults. They were well-known and well-liked in the community, yet they were not flashy or ostentatious. They lived a very comfortable lifestyle, and never wanted for anything, but they lived below their means. They kept the same cars and furniture for years and years, but they always looked new because they cared for them. They stayed in the same jobs for the entirety of their careers and both rose to management level. They raised two great kids and sent them to college. Their only major move was to move from the neighborhood in which they had lived for four decades to be close to their grandchildren. What was their sacrifice? They sacrificed self for others. *They sacrificed more for just enough.* They sacrificed glory and accolades for quiet respect and a humble home. By honoring God, they were blessed with His enveloping love and protection...and God provided just what they needed at the right time and the right place.

The devil's playground is instability and uncertainty. The more that you can hold on to what is important-God, family and friends; the less likely that you will succumb to the devil's attack. Make your nest a refuge of comfort and peace, fortified by impenetrable walls from those who wish to see you perish and fail. Simpler IS better. This is a very hard lesson for young people to learn today as it was when I was young. If I had chosen a simpler lifestyle, there is no doubt that I would have been a happier and better person. *God could care less what you have. He only cares about who you are. Remember that as you build your nests.*

Questions and Notes

1.   What are the reasons for you to build a nest even at a young age?
2.   Why are people who live simpler, consistent lives happier than other people? How is their focus different from people who are nomadic?
3.   Would our society be better if more people built their nests? Why?

Lessons From Grandpa

I miss Grandpa. He was a man of paradox. He was a simple man, yet he had a deeply complex life at times. He was a slightly above average student, but he accomplished the pinnacle of success by achieving his doctorate in education. Being a single child, he was often shy in social situations, yet he loved his family and he enjoyed hanging out with his billiard buddies. He was a decorated combat veteran who never spoke of his wartime experiences.

Because Grandpa was a single child, he didn't develop functional social skills until he was well into his middle-age years. When he returned from his last tour of duty in Vietnam, he was hardened by years of combat experience, and it took him years to soften. Unfortunately, these were my formative years. Needless to say, my relationship with him during those years was tepid, at best. It was only after the hands of time had made many turns that he began to be engaging. It began after he suffered some heart problems. Like most men who are honed and chiseled on the battlefield, he felt invincible. But, when the heart attacks started coming and he could see his children leaving the nest to start their lives, I believe that he had a spiritual epiphany. He became kind, loving and generous. Nobody had a harsh word to say about Max Wade Garoutte.

The coup de gras was when he started to experience the joy of grandchildren. Oh, how he loved them! The edge that had been sharpened by war was gone and he adored his grandchildren. Although I never asked him, I believe that he was making up for his deficiencies when he was a young father. The Lord had blessed him with beautiful, healthy grandchildren and he seized the precious time with them to a adore them and give thanks that He, the Heavenly Father, had said, "yes, I will" to Dad's prayer for a second chance.

My prayer for each of you is that you will make the most of all your opportunities, and as a loving parent, that I can support and protect you the very best I can. Grandpa made me understand the importance of this principle. I have tried to do the best I can...to honor you, my earthly Father and my Heavenly Father. However, when I fail and stumble, I have prayed as my father did to have a second chance. There will be a day after I am gone from this earth that you will take time to reflect. I hope that you can review my life, my personality, my attributes and my accomplishments. *I pray that in your hearts, you will understand that my beloved sons are among my greatest accomplishments and that you will also be men of paradox like Jesus and your Grandpa were.*

Questions and Notes

1. *Why are we referred to as children of God?*

2. *How has life's ups and downs changed you thus far? Has it been for the better or worse? Why?*

3. *We worship a God of second chances. How has God given you a second chance?*

Find Your "Sweet Spot"

Max Lucado, the other Max, wrote about finding your "sweet spot" in one of his books. He couldn't have been more correct. God gives all of us gifts-spiritual and otherwise. He gives some of his children more than others, but he does not give all gifts to one person. Why? He wants us to live in relationship with each other in a community where we have shared responsibilities and spiritual interdependence. He wants us to be in relationship with others, and totally dependent on Him. My prayer for you is that you will begin very early to recognize your gifts and start developing them. Yes, it is possible to overachieve in a way that you can develop yourself outside your range of gifts, but it is *much* more difficult. *You will recognize your gifts by that which comes easy to you. Unfortunately, these are the exact traits that we take for granted and tend to under-develop. By giving you gifts, God is, in essence, giving you a head-start. It is also His way of pushing you in the direction that He wants you to go.* Obviously, by having a head-start, if you work diligently, you can achieve more.

You each have been blessed with so many gifts. As a proud dad, I believe that you have more than average gifts. I have tried to point these out to you. Sometimes, I am subtle, and other times, not. I did this because I recognized that God is giving you a hint and direction on where he wants your life path to go. It is a little bit like having training wheels on your bike. They keep you from falling and align you in a relatively straight path. Out of your sight, God is behind you gently pushing you. When you gain confidence the training wheels come up, and eventually off. From there, it is up to you, and your obedience to His instruction, that will determine your direction. Your free will may take you in a direction that is contrary to God's...and you may even crash. But, God will always be there to pick you up and set you back on you're the right path if you follow His guidance.

Questions and Notes

1. *What are your "sweet spots?"*
2. *Are you maximizing the gifts that you have been given? If not, why?*
3. *If you are pursuing a vocation or avocation that is not in your "sweet spot," should you? What can you expect if you challenge yourself outside of your sweet spot? Should this discourage you?*
4. *Make a list of your spiritual gifts and talents. Consider how these gifts and talents will align with your life goals.*

Dealing With Despair and Disappointment

Aside from personal experience, you will find in your lives that observing those around you, and how they respond to adversity, can provide great life lessons. I have learned a valuable life lesson from your grandparents, Big Daddy and Mimi. This is a lesson that I would never want to endure personally. Your grandparents lost their only son, Danny, to a tragic event. By all accounts, Danny had everything going for him, and yet, God allowed circumstances that led to his death. Big Daddy and Mimi have suffered immeasurably. Children are supposed to outlive their parents. I am sure that the suffering they have endured as a result of this loss has been sustained, although perhaps, moderated with time. Parents who have endured the loss of a child often experience anger, guilt and remorse. They are haunted by the most perplexing and elusive question...why did this happen? The "why" questions, especially the ones having to do with life's adversity and challenges, are the hardest to reconcile. As a physician, I have asked this question many times in my career. Rarely, am I able to thoughtfully rationalize the answer. Some questions are left to be answered when we pass from this life and sit at the throne of God to understand His purpose for allowing bad things to happen to good people.

I never, ever want to experience the immense pain that your grandparents have had. However, as a physician, I can certainly empathize with them. I have consoled many a patient who has lost a child. I have learned that mourning is a process. It can't be rushed and it is a gateway to healing. Like most wounds, there will be healing, but there also will be a scar that will only vanish when we are rejoined with our loved ones. Here are some points of consideration should you ever experience profound loss whether it is from death or other life circumstances.

- When you lose someone, hold on to your earthly relationships-especially with those who share your deep remorse regarding your loss.
- Focus up and out, not down and in. When you are in your deepest pain, try to divert your energy toward God's plans particularly as it impacts helping others. Our natural tendency during pain is to withdraw and recoil. Quiet

time is natural during an emotional departure, but don't let solace suffocate you. God will speak to you through other godly people. He can't do that if you withdraw from interpersonal connection.

- Pray incessantly. We honor and praise a loving God. He WILL grant you peace and healing...but in His perfect time.

- Appreciate that it is not your place to understand all things.

- Seek out others who have experienced similar pain and who have progressed farther in the healing process. They have credibility and insight that they will share if you ask.

- Give thanks in ALL things. Not for the tragedy, but for what gifts and opportunities that God may present as a result of them.

- Painful life events are the mallet and God provides the chisel. Major events may dramatically shape your character. Leave it to Him to decide the direction and size of the cuts while He continues to mold, shape and refine you.

- Realize that the most difficult answers are to the "why" questions...many of which will not be answered while you live on earth.

Questions and Notes

1. *What is the best way to comfort someone in their time of loss? What should you say and what shouldn't you say?*

2. *What will you do when you experience profound tragedy? How will you respond?*

Courage To Surrender

Cowardliness has been associated with surrender, but this is not true. In your life, there will be times that you will find it best to surrender to adversity. Running from adversity is cowardliness. Surrender actually requires more courage than fighting often does. With surrender, you are placing yourself at the mercy of your adversary. Obviously, if your enemy intends to dispatch you, your best options are to run or fight. However, in life's battleground, there are times when surrender is best-especially if your opponent is capable of mercy.

One of your most difficult decisions will be when to fight, when to run and when to surrender. Fighting an un-winnable fight is fruitless. It may be better to surrender so that you can fight another day.

The ultimate example of surrender was Christ's sacrifice. Even in the Garden of Gethsemane, Christ questioned whether surrender was really what God wanted. His courage in surrender was self-evident. Sacrifice on behalf of others brings honor to you and is one of the greatest gifts that you can give our Heavenly Father.

Questions and Notes

1. *Why have we been taught that it is cowardly to surrender? Is this correct?*

2. *Have you had a time when you should have surrendered instead of fought? If so, how do you think the outcome would have changed if you had surrendered?*

3. *What areas do you see in the life ahead of you where you may have to choose to fight or surrender? How can you prepare for those times now?*

The Joy of Fatherhood

There is no way that I can adequately explain the absolute joy that it has been to be your father. Being a dad to a son is God's way of giving us a glimpse of His elation to have a son who once walked this earth, and who gave the ultimate sacrifice for us. I cannot imagine being Abraham when he walked with his son, Isaac, knowing that God was calling him to sacrifice him. What a testament in faith! Frankly, the happiness and joy and thankfulness to have all of you as my sons bring overwhelming emotion. While you are young adults, I don't expect you to understand this. The light bulb will only turn on when you are able to gaze into your son's or daughter's eyes and know that they are yours forever. The pure pleasure of watching you grow and mature is unexplainable. Bryce, even though we kidded that you promised that you would "stay small." I knew that you would grow into a man. This is bittersweet, but mostly sweet. You see; we "rent" our kids.

Bryce and Braden, I am so proud of you for the courage and strength that you showed when we were displaced by divorce. I want you to know that I really tried to make the right decisions even though they might not have felt right at the time. I believe God's validation that the decision was correct, albeit painful, is that he honored me with the wonderful gift of having Meg and Tristan come into my life. Although I know, at first, it was difficult for you both; I hope that you now understand that this was part of God's plan. Your brother, Tristan, has thrived in his environment with you as his brothers. Meg, who is such a godly wife and mother, accepted you both as her own from day one. For that, we must all be thankful because many times it is not the case in "blended families."

Tristan, you have an emotional maturity beyond your years and you have been unbelievably accepting and adaptive under extremely challenging circumstances. Just as your mother accepted Bryce and Braden immediately, so did you. For that, I am forever grateful.

As you grow, and mature, and experience life, I pray that you will marry a godly wife who respects you for whom you are and that one day you will share the immense pleasure of fatherhood. Only then, will you fully appreciate my joy and gratitude for being a father to all my sons.

Questions and Notes

1. *Visualize the children that you wish to have. Write down their characteristics. Why have you selected those attributes? What will you do if your children are different from your "ideal child?"*

2. *How will you be a different parent to your children as compared to your parents have been to you? Why?*

Dad's Words of Advice

Respect-show it, and it will be shown to you.

Discretion-have it, so that others may keep your secrets as well.

Forgiveness-practice it, even when it is difficult.

Empathy-demonstrate it, so you may have it when you need it.

Courtesy-show it, for others even when they don't reciprocate.

Thankfulness-practice it, especially when it is difficult.

Happiness-seek it, and live it.

Honor-people, your body and God.

Create-opportunities, art and music, healthy relationships.

Generosity-show it always, but especially if you have more than you need.

Beauty-see it in everyone and everything that God has made.

Listen-intently, and with quiet reserve and contemplation.

Pleasure-may you have it, but more importantly give it.

Humility-develop it, despite your accomplishments.

Peace-may you experience that which passes all understanding.

LOVE-always.

Questions and Notes

1. *As a parent, what would you add to the Words of Advice list? Why?*

Epilogue

I love you guys more than you can know...at least until you are a dad and you become overwhelmed with love for your children. Isn't it strange that one weekend while sitting in the house alone I heard the quiet whisper that said that I should write this small book. Of course, the whisper was from the Great Whisperer, so I hope that reading this little book of fatherly advice will breathe God's power and purpose through you. I will not always be here on earth for you, but I will always be with you...in spirit, in my legacy and in the writings of this manuscript. You see, this book of instruction is really a love letter from a dad to his sons. Just as the Bible was a love letter to us. God wants the best for you-as do I. I know that you are each capable of great things in your own, very special ways. Great things may not be fame or fortune. It certainly isn't in God's eyes. You have been given a great education, and your parents have tried to instill the love of God, and the importance of having Him, in your life. We want you to follow His instructions to you as revealed in the Bible, and you should always know that *His way is the best way* even if it takes you down a path that differs from where your free-will wants to take you.

This book will likely sit on your bookshelf or in a drawer during your life. Perhaps, when you have sons and daughters, you will share it with them. My prayer is that when you are struggling, or lonesome, or sad; you will pick up this book and know that I am with you in loving and adoring splendor....because I will be.

Love always,
Dad

Fatherly Advice
"A Father's Dreams, Hopes and Advice for His Sons"

Max Gerald Garoutte, M.D., is a board-certified internist and cardiologist currently practicing in San Antonio, Texas. He has enjoyed a long and prosperous career in service of his patients since 1986. He has practiced in the areas of general internal medicine, general cardiology, non-invasive/invasive/interventional cardiology. His special interests are prevention and wellness.

Dr. Garoutte was born in central Missouri. He discovered at an early age that he had a passion for medicine. After graduating from high school at the age of 16, he spent the next eight years achieving his undergraduate degree and medical degree at the University of Missouri-Columbia. After completing his residency and fellowship, he moved to his adopted home state of Texas where he has been practicing for the three decades.

His father, Max Wade, served his country honorably as a three tour combat veteran. He was a decorated soldier who received the rank of Lieutenant Colonel prior to his retirement. He was recognized for his valor in combat by receiving two Bronze Stars. After returning from Vietnam, he attained his doctorate in education from the University of Missouri. Max Wade Garoutte, EdD, Lt. Col. (ret) went to be with his Heavenly Father on January, 26, 2007.

Max Gerald lives with his wonderful wife, and best supporter, Meg, in their home in San Antonio. Bryce Connor is attending Baylor University and is pursuing a business degree. Prior to matriculating into Baylor, Bryce received his high schools' recognition as the top all-around student. Tristan Joseph is currently a student at one of the pre-eminent college preparatory schools in San Antonio. He will be playing Division 1 lacrosse at Furman University while he pursues his college studies. Braden Kyle is an accomplished student and is interested in pursuing a career in engineering. He has also achieved the prestigious rank of Eagle Scout.

Dr. Garoutte and his family enjoy spending time at their M&M River Ranch in Colorado. They are all avid scuba divers and enjoy outdoor activities such as hiking and skiing/snowboarding. Dr. Garoutte enjoys music, painting, writing prose and poetry and fly fishing.

Max and Meg look forward to retirement on their beautiful Colorado River Ranch where they will entertain their friends, family, children and one day....grandchildren.

Max Gerald, "Doctor Max," has been the author of three books, *Maximum Destiny, Maximum Destiny Workbook* and *Saving Medicine.* He is currently working on his first novel to be published soon. More information can be found at maximumdestiny.com.

$14.95

www.ingramcontent.com/pod-product-compliance
Lightning Source LLC
LaVergne TN
LVHW091157080426
835509LV00006B/737